The Beginners Guide to Residential Rental Property.

(How to set up a 5-10 house business)

The short guide to get you started and help answer commonly asked questions.

-Contents-

About the Author

Before you begin check list

Chapter 1 – The set up

Chapter 2 – LLC

Chapter 3 – Money

Chapter 4 – Realtors, Property managers, Title companies

Chapter 5 – Handyman and other trades

Chapter 6 – Mentor

Chapter 7 – The process

Chapter 8 – Bullet proof

Chapter 9 – Warning / Final thoughts

Additional Notes

About the Author

My name is Shane Robb I live in Oklahoma with my Wife and three daughters. By trade I am an electrical contractor. I have always ventured into other profitable possibilities. A few years back I decided to check into real estate investment opportunities. In my journey I have met some fantastic people and learned some valuable lessons which I will pass on in this book. My goal is to offer others what I couldn't find in a book. Experience. My real estate mentor Mr. G was willing to pour into my life and help me avoid pitfalls and set up a successful small rental business. He provided me with the experience that couldn't be found elsewhere. Thank you Mr. G!!

My Myers-Briggs Code (ESTJ)

Before You Begin Check List

1.) Are you (good) with money?
- Yes... Proceed
- No... Read one of Dave Ramsey's books on financial peace. (or something similar) You need your finances in order before you proceed.

2.) Do you know your Myers-Briggs Type/code?
- Yes... proceed
- No.. Take the Myers-Briggs test online (its free) then proceed.

3.) Is your spouse, mentor, advisor, in support of your decision?
- Yes.. Proceed
- No.. Find out what is holding them back ... listen... if you still wish to proceed, do so with caution.

Once you answered Yes to these questions proceed........

This book is a simple yet effective and direct guide to setting up a small (5-10) rental property business. So you may be wondering what the questions at the beginning of the book are for? The short answer because they matter. If you're bad with money, don't understand or know your core values, strengths and weaknesses. If you fail to have a support system in place…. You are planning to fail. I don't wish to see anyone fail, not to say you won't regardless. Having these things in order increase the likely hood for success. This business like any depend on three core principles. Be intentional, accountability, be consistent. The intent for this book is to inspire, motivate, and inform others about the residential rental business. Let's begin.

Chapter 1

The set up

In order to get started in this business you are going to need to acquire the following. Set up an LLC, Have $20-30K Cash on hand(depends on your market area), Bankers willing to help you out with LOC(line Of Credit) and Loans, Title Company, Property Manager, Realtors, Handyman, and other trade contacts. Find a real estate mentor already doing this business willing to help you and answer questions. As we walk through this book we will cover the importance of each item mentioned above. So if you're ready lets dive in!

Chapter 2

LLC

You are starting a "business" so you have to treat it like one. Setting up an LLC is fairly simple. You should be able to contact your secretary of state office and someone can give you the directions for setting up a basic LLC. If you find this too much work or difficult to do most attorneys can set one up for a few hundred dollars (just shop around). The LLC gives you an extra layer of protection which you will want long term. It also look better to the banks. My recommendation is do not name the LLC after yourself, I know you may be proud but, if your wanting to stay incognito pick a different name _____ Properties, investments, Rentals, something just not your name. This will make sense in later chapters.

Chapter 3

Money

If you're good with money or have learned to become good with money, you should have some cash saved up. I used $20-30k for the Oklahoma area (cash on hand amount may differ depending on your market area). The target home price for this model is $50-$70k. The cash on hand gives you a good cushion to get in the door with the banks. When you go to the banks to start shopping look for the small banks. They are the ones more likely to help you out. Big commercial big name banks typically try to fit you in a box and usually not "investor friendly", at least on the small business side. When you find your bank you need to set up a LOC (line of credit) you many need to use your personal home or any other assets if needed. No risk.. No reward.. Get the biggest LOC possible with the longest term possible. I started out with $75K. Most banks can go up to 99K without to many hoops to jump through (once you exceed that amount cost goes up and more paper work is involved). Once your LOC is set up your ready to start looking for your first property. LOC allows you to be a "Cash buyer" which allows you to get deals below market. Timing is important, for instance. The end of the year banks are needing to clear their books of any REO properties, they are more willing to take lower offers at this time giving you the "cash buyer" more leverage. Banks love "cash buyers" less hoops to jump through.

Chapter 4
Realtors, Property Managers, Title companies.

Realtors) when you begin to the search for your first property most people tend to use the same realtor to buy/sell everything they do. That is great but, not if you want a deal. A realtor's main job is to "Sell" a home. So if you bring in another realtor in on a deal the listing realtor loses half their paycheck! I don't know about you but that doesn't sound ideal if I were the listing realtor. So for this situation try to use the listing realtor. They will be more likely to help you "get the deal" by working direct with them allowing them to make the full paycheck. Using this method also provides you with multiple realtor contacts, which long term can lead to more opportunities.
Title Companies) Another crucial contact. Find a title company to work with. Unlike

Realtors you will want to try and be exclusive. Get to know the staff well. You will want to use the same company for all transactions if possible. The more loyal you are, the better they will treat you with fees etc. Most of the time you get to choose where to close

Property Managers) I recommend finding at least 2 good ones. In order to be successful you need your time. If you are busy answering phone and trying to fix every little issue that may come up, rent properties, evict people. Etc.. Then when do you have time to purchase/look for more properties? It's a business, so treat it like one. A property manager is a key asset. They are in charge of all the things listed above. Trust me you don't want a tenant calling you in the middle of the night about a clogged toilet, They Will! A property manager lets you be anonymous. They charge a minimum monthly fee (which in most cases is a tax write off) but, it is well worth it. The reason for having at least 2 on hand? When you have an empty property there is strength in numbers. When there is competition your property rents faster. An empty property is lost money! I have had properties sit for 3-4 months! This is not good. So always have a few property managers on hand, plus it's never good to have all your eggs in one basket.

Chapter 5

Handyman and other trades

When you purchase a property you will most likely need to do some repairs to get it rent ready. A general handyman can do most minor repairs, paint, door locks, trim, minor electrical and plumbing, etc. For bigger projects/repairs you will need skilled tradesmen. These contacts can be acquired by your property manager (see the value), mentor, realtors, bankers, etc. Your property manager can handle contracting the repairs for you in most cases. Important note: washers/dryers, refrigerators, dishwashers, and disposals are all luxury items, not necessity items. The general rule of thumb "if you supply it, you repair/replace it" If you want to be ahead of the repair and maintenance game avoid supplying these items if possible.

Chapter 6

Mentor

If ye seek, ye shall find a mentor. It's important to find someone in the business that can help avoid pit falls. There are plenty of people in your area that are in the rental property business. Your job is to find them. Look for community events, online, chamber of commerce etc. A mentor is crucial, they can cheer you on in the highs and lows. They can give you suggestions and valuable information not found in a book. Experience. Sometimes they can turn you onto deals you would not have known about. If it were not for my mentor Mr. G, I would not have made it very far in the rental business. Through our relationship we inspired and motivated one another. When I wanted to give up I could look at his business/success and regain hope. This Business can be tough at times. It helps to have a source of encouragement to reflect upon. Thank you Mr. G!

Chapter 7

The Process

We have covered the basics. Now let's run through a scenario together. You have secured you LOC, you find a property worth buying that meets your criteria. You contact the "listing realtor", make the Cash offer. If accepted you contact "your" title company and get the closing process started. Once you close on the property, meet with you handyman to assess repairs needed to make the property rent ready. Once the property is rent ready contact your property manager to start the listing. If the house is not rented in 1 week or at least doesn't have high traffic, bring in the additional property manager. A little competition will get it rented. Winner gets your business (on that property). Once rented go to your banker and request a loan for the property so you can pay off your LOC. If you bought right you may have enough equity to get a loan without much out of pocket expense. Most investment loans are 75-80% LTV (Loan to value) leaving you to either have 20% equity in the property or investing the difference. Once the loan if closed and the LOC is cleared.. save some cash and repeat the process. As you acquire more properties you can consolidate loans to save on monthly payments. Buying rental properties is like buying stocks you don't make a ton with 1-2 shares.. The more you acquire the more you make. Remember you acquire more risk! No risk, No reward. Rental business is good when it's good and, bad when its bad but, if you can be intentional and eliminate as many possible problems upfront, it's much easier to deal with long term. Note: if you are able to purchase multiple properties at once through package deals sometimes that can help you achieve your goal faster (not easier, just faster). In the next chapter I'll go over a few thoughts of what can be done to make the rental process less problematic.

Chapter 8

Bullet Proof

One thing to think about is how to make your properties bullet proof. Think of anything that could be broken and make a list. Ceiling fans, electrical outlets, plumbing shut off valves, etc. The best thing to do is eliminate potential problems before they happen. When I go into a house I change out all the switches and outlets, plumbing shut off valves, light fixtures, remove dishwashers, remove garbage disposals, remove any appliances that are not required, and try simplify each house as much as possible. If you can convert the property to total electric do it. This eliminates all the hazards that can come with natural gas. Also in Oklahoma natural gas is the only utility that really hammers tenants with large deposits in order to turn the service on. If you are painting try to use the same color paint and brand for every house, due that same thing for carpet and other flooring. I'd even recommend the same light fixtures and counter tops. The goal here is to make each property the same. If each property is set up the same then you don't have to remember what paint color you used, what flooring to match etc... Ceiling fans get broken constantly so I try to limit them to the living room and master bedroom. Its little things like this that make the process go so much smoother. You want to keep each property as nice as possible for people. If you are not willing to spend the money upfront to make the house nice, you will end up spending it in repairs later.

Chapter 9

Warning / Final Thoughts

So my upfront warning. Things will break, sometimes on their own, sometimes tenants will damage or break things. You have to be ready financially and mentally. Make sure to have good insurance policies that cover theft and vandalism (most don't, it's an endorsement). I have had toilets clog, tree roots get into plumbing lines, hot water tanks need replacement, Roofs need repair, A/C units need repair (even stolen!), and one house the entire electrical was stripped out! I don't tell you this to scare you but to warn you. These are things that happen, you have to be ready. I would keep majority of the rental proceeds back for these unknown situations. Once you have a few rental properties paid off, you will have a better gauge of how much money you want to keep back for repairs etc. Unless you have cash to pay off 5-10 properties upfront, the rental property business is a long term investment. Most people's goal it to have all properties paid and producing a monthly income for retirement. However I heard a saying that "Retirement is not an age.. It's an income". So with that said the faster you can pay them off, the faster you can retire, if that's what you choose to do. It's never as easy as it sounds...LOL...No one can do this for you, you have to choose to do it.

Hope you have a Fantastic Adventure!

Additional Notes

- Things will break/need repairs
  (Plan on it / make a budget)
- People will move out
  (Except it/be ready/prepared)
- Always Have a property manager
- Always have an emergency fund!
- Find reliable handyman/tradesmen
- Change air filters min./every 3-mo.
- Total Electric is best choice if possible
- Anything extra (dishwasher, washer/dryer, microwave, etc.) is on you when it breaks. Avoid these items if possible.
- Have an LOC and plenty bankers on your side, opportunities will come, you must be ready, strike while the iron is hot.
- Keep properties close together if possible.

Contact List

Notes

www.ingramcontent.com/pod-product-compliance
Lightning Source LLC
Chambersburg PA
CBHW031601210526
45464CB00003B/1383